AmericanGirl Library®

Paper Clip
Jewelry!

By Kelli Peduzzi

Published by Pleasant Company Publications
Text Copyright © 2000 by Kelli Peduzzi
Photography, Illustrations Copyright © 2000 by American Girl, LLC

Questions or comments?
Call 1-800-845-0005, visit our Web site at **americangirl.com**,
or write American Girl, P.O. Box 620497, Middleton, WI 53562-0497.

Manufactured in China.
04 05 06 07 08 09 C&C 10 09 08 07 06 05 04 03 02

American Girl Library® and American Girl® are registered trademarks
of American Girl, LLC.

Editorial Development: Trula Magruder, Michelle Watkins
Art Direction and Design: Chris Lorette David, Camela Decaire
Model Photography: Sandy May
Tabletop Photography: James H. Young
Jewelry Styling: Demetra Saloutos-Motz, Sarajane V. Lien
Illustration: Susan Spellman

The author dedicates this book in memory of Sylvia Smook,
with special thanks to Diane Smook, Tiffany Schneck, and Nancy Phillips.

ISBN 1-58485-965-2

Dear Reader,

Within these pages, you'll discover dozens of different ways to turn ordinary paper clips into **amazing jewelry,** room **accessories,** and gifts, too!

Learn the basic wire-working skills used by professional jewelers. Then **create designs** that fit your style. Go dressy, go casual, or invent a unique look!

The **starter kit** includes enough clips, beads, and jewelry fittings to get you going, and you'll be able to use your personal pair of jewelry pliers again and again.

Need a fashion tip? **Dress up a paper clip!**

Your friends at *American Girl*

BASICS

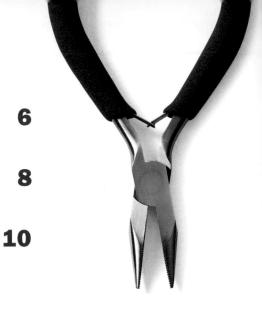

Contents

PROJECTS

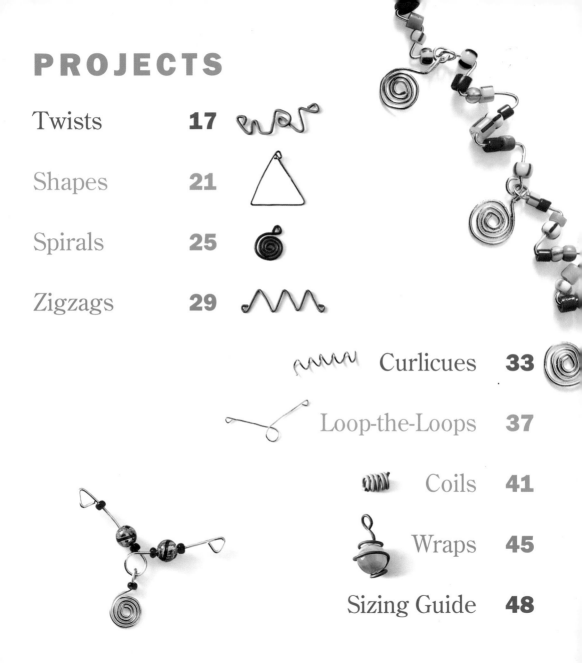

Your Tools

Get to know your tools **before you start.**

Important!

Keep small items out of a younger child's hands—and mouth. Kids can choke on little things like beads, so be sure everything's stored safely. Keep pliers, in particular, in a safe place to prevent kids from seriously hurting themselves and others.

Adult supervision is recommended when using pliers.

Work Area

Prevent tired arms, shoulders, and eyes by working at a table that is waist high and well lit. Keep beads and smaller items from falling to the floor by laying them in a shoe box lid or on a piece of fabric, a paper towel, or a paper plate.

Work Order

Projects in this book go from very simple to more challenging. Each project builds on a previous one, so it's best to work from the beginning. After you leave **BASICS**, new skills are explained in boxes. They're titled **PRACTICE THIS FIRST** because you get a better result if you try those skills before starting the projects.

String

When a project calls for string, you can use thread, cord, or elastic—anything that's strong enough to hold beads, fits through bead holes, doesn't kink, and if visible, is stylish.

Beads

When your bead supply runs low, you can find a good selection at craft, bead, and sewing stores. Bring a paper clip with you to slip through the bead holes so you can make sure the beads you choose will work.

When beading a long strand of paper clips or string, keep it from tangling by taping one end to your work surface.

Clasps

A clasp can be anything that holds jewelry ends together—a knot, a metal fastener, or even a paper clip. To use the ring clasps provided, tie the string ends through the clasp loops, then knot the string.

Pliers

Needle-nose pliers act like strong fingers. They grip, bend, and straighten wire. If you lay the plier handles flat in your palm and squeeze your fingers closed, the pliers will close, too. Like fingers, pliers can pinch, so pay attention to what you're doing when working with them. Be sure to ask an adult to show you how to handle the pliers if you aren't sure how they work.

Paper Clips

Avoid using paper clips that are hard to bend. Plastic-coated clips are easiest to work with, then gold, and finally, silver.

Hands

When making jewelry, hands do most of the work, so treat them kindly. If they feel tired from bending too many paper clips, give them a break. To stretch your hands, squeeze your fists closed, then open them wide. Repeat as needed.

7

Add a Charm

Put all your funky, silly, and **special charms** to work!

Clip-Its

Add personality to your paper-work! Slide a charm, button, or bead on a paper clip, then clip it to invitations, reports, memos, and more.

Dear Amy,
I was shopping in the mall and saw this cute charm! It reminded me of you. I wish I could give it in

The Bengal Tige
by Kelsey Jackson

endangered species
Their scientific na
of tiger left in
claws, whisk

: they
. The
The

Mom,
't forget to
up after

Do-Drops

Dangle these colorful pins from anything you carry! Slip beads and charms along 1 side of the paper clips, then slip the clips on a safety pin. Attach pins to jackets, hats, purses, or backpacks.

Begin with Bends

Make **simple bends** to create a clever chain.

1 Slip a bead on the inside leg of a paper clip. Hold the clip tightly in one hand, and use the pliers to bend the tip of the leg out 90 degrees. This will keep the bead on the clip.

2 Bend the outside leg of the clip in 90 degrees. Make as many clips as you'll need, then slide them together, creating a chain of the desired length.

Option: Add lots of beads to a paper clip before bending the legs closed.

Knickknack Basket

Turn a plain basket into a unique hanging bin. Following the directions shown at left, use large paper clips to make 3 chains of equal length. Hook one end of each chain to the top of a wire basket. (Space chains evenly apart.) Hook the other end to a large paper clip. Slip the clip over a ceiling hook, then fill the basket with hair accessories or lightweight knickknacks.

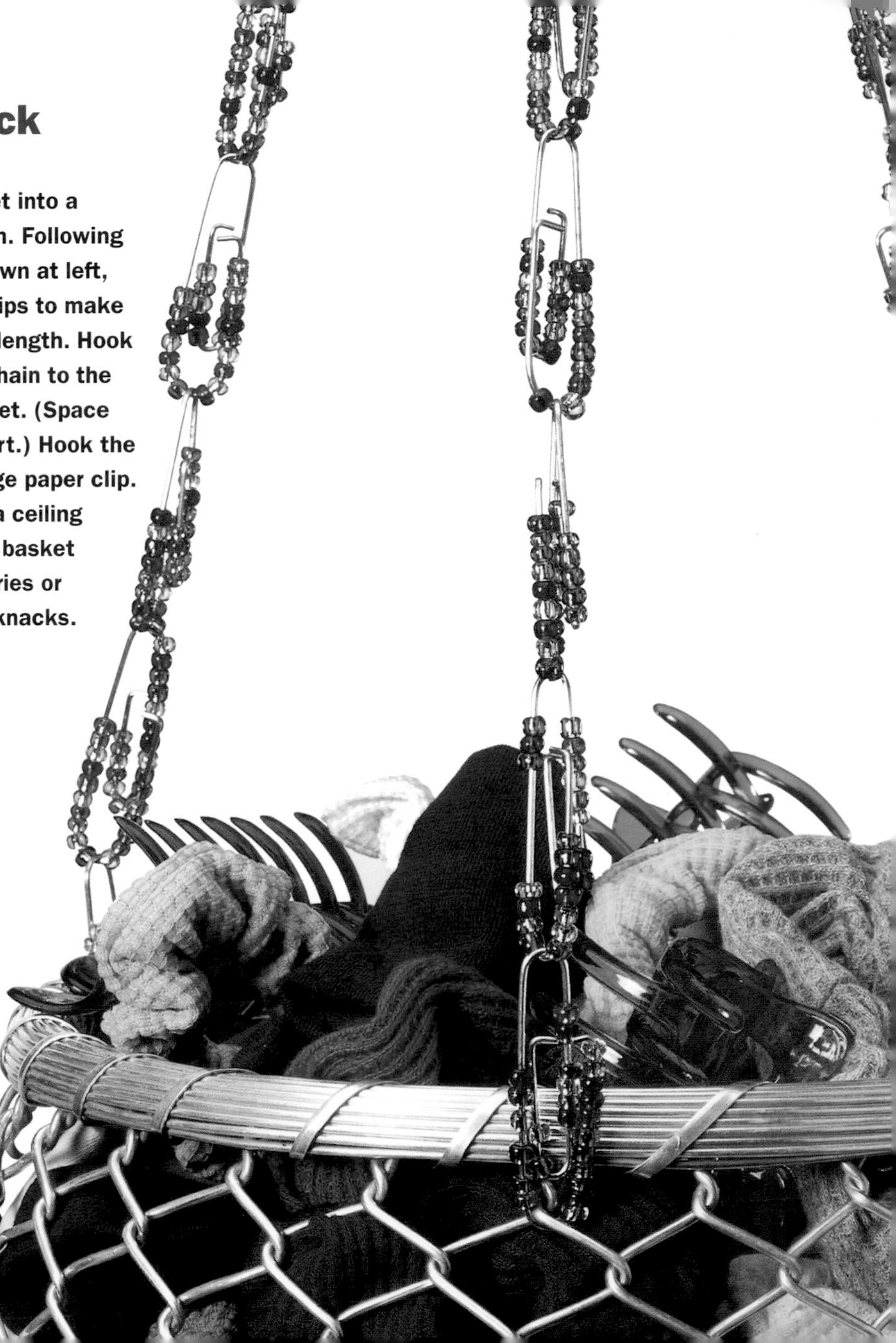

Get It Straight

Straightening your paper clip is the first step to **super style!**

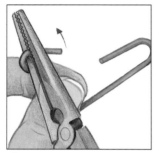

1 With your fingers, spread a paper clip into a wide V. Place the pliers just before the first bend, as shown above.

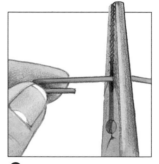

2 To straighten the clip, squeeze the pliers tightly, open them, move them a bit along the bend, then squeeze them again. Gently lift the clip straight with your fingers as you're squeezing. Continue to do this over each bend until the clip is flat.

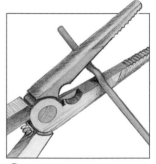

3 Look at the clip closely. If you see any small bends, squeeze them flat.

Twist and turn a clip to make fun designs.

Instead of beads, add charms.

Finger Fashion

Try both a bead and a charm.

1 To make a basic ring, first straighten a paper clip. Then use your fingers to bend the clip around a finger-sized object, such as a thick marker.

2 Crisscross the ends over the marker, make a twist, then slide the ring off.

3 Slip a bead on each end, then bend the tips under the beads. Adjust the position of the beads with your fingers or pliers.

Learn to Loop

Clasping, dangling, linking, and other **jewelry making** begins with a little loop.

Make a Loop

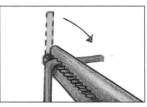

1 Straighten a paper clip, then grip the end of the clip with the plier tips and make a 90-degree bend.

2 Put the pliers just behind the bend, and sharply turn the clip to close the loop. Each time a loop is used at a clip end, it will be called an "end loop."

Open a Loop

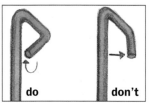

do   don't

1 Imagine a loop lying flat on a table. To open it, you would lift the loop bottom up off the table—not pull it sideways. To practice, hold a loop in your hand and open it with pliers.

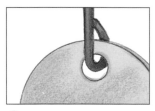

2 Slide a charm, bead, or zipper on the loop, then bend it back into place. Reclose the gap completely.

Hip Zips

Design a zipper pull that's classy, cute, or cool! First straighten a paper clip, then make an end loop. Slide on beads or charms, but leave enough room to make a small loop at the other end. To attach the zipper pull, reopen the top end loop, slip the pull on the zipper, then reclose.

Jewelry Tips

Now that you've mastered jewelry-making basics, study these **simple tips** for success!

To prevent scratches to the paper clips, wrap plier tips with tape.

Dab string ends and all knots with clear nail polish, and let dry completely.

If a project's suggested length doesn't fit you, add or remove clips.

Use twice as much string as you think you'll need, so you'll have extra to tie knots. Always trim string close to the knots.

Before tying the final knots, try the jewelry on in front of a mirror to see if it hangs correctly. Then mark the strings where your clasp should go.

Twists

Twist and turn, tangle and bend
a paper clip from end to end.

Wrist Twists

Making a Twist

1 Straighten a paper clip, then use the pliers to make an end loop.

2 Turn the clip in any direction or wrap it around a small object, such as a nail, to create unusual twists.

3 Loop the other end closed.

YOU WILL NEED

- 6 silver paper clips
- Pliers
- Small object, such as a nail, if desired
- 5 charms
- Clasp

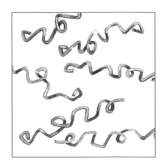

1 Create 6 twists, following the instructions shown at left.

Dress it up, dress it down. Put **your own twist** on this silvery bracelet!

2 Reopen the end loop of a clip, and attach it to the end loop of another one. Repeat with remaining twists.

3 Open the loop on a charm, and attach it where 2 end loops connect. Repeat with remaining charms.

4 To attach the clasp, open a loop on one end, slip in the clasp loop, and reclose. Repeat on the opposite side.

Twisty Treasures

Dancing Wire

To make this necklace, slip glass beads on twists, then bend the tiniest end loops you can. Connect the end loops until the necklace is long enough to slip over your head.

Light Show

Give this elegant candle as a gift, and watch it light up a smile! To begin, slip glass beads on silver twists. Don't add end loops! Instead, heat clip ends in hot tap water so they can be pressed into the candle without chipping it.

Shapes

Style a triangle, design a square—
give simple shapes fashion flair!

Triangle Dangle

Making a Triangle

1 Straighten a paper clip, then bend an end loop.

triangle template

2 Lay the clip along the template above. With a marker, put a line on the clip at the dot. Bend at the mark. Repeat with the next dot.

3 Make another end loop, reopen it, slip in the first loop, and reclose.

YOU WILL NEED

- **1 silver paper clip**
- **Pliers**
- **Marker**
- **Beads and charms**
- **String**

1 Follow the directions in steps 1 and 2 shown at left, but before making the first bend, add beads up to the mark.

Let your imagination **soar to new heights** when styling a triangle—a shape as ancient as the mountains.

2 Bend the clip at the mark, then add more beads. (Add a single charm, if desired, so it's centered at the bottom.) Make another bend, and add the remaining beads.

3 Follow the instructions in step 3 shown at left, then thread the string through a loop and tie the loose ends into a knot, so it will slip over your head.

Spiraling Squares

Go ahead and be square! Turn a **classic shape** into a contemporary creation.

1 Straighten a paper clip, then bend an end loop. Starting ¼ inch from the loop, make a bend. Continue making bends farther and farther apart. Finally, add an end loop.

2 Make another square. Open the end loop of the first square, slip in the edge of the second, and reclose. Repeat with enough squares to fit around your wrist.

3 To add a clasp, open the last end loop, slip in the clasp loop, and reclose. At the opposite end, open the clasp ring, slip in the edge of the square, and reclose.

Spirals

A spin, a twirl, a wire swirl. Exotic, hypnotic—
and looks like you bought it!

Silvery Swirls

Making a Spiral

1 Straighten a paper clip. Bend a tiny loop and clamp it in the pliers so the clip points out the side. While tightly squeezing the pliers, push the clip up.

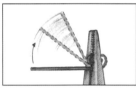

2 Reposition the clip in the pliers so it points to the side. Push the clip up. Repeat until you're left with a ½-inch tail.

3 Make an end loop with the tail. Use your pliers to turn the loop at a right angle to the spiral so it will dangle.

YOU WILL NEED

- **7 silver paper clips**
- **Pliers**
- **2 feet of string**
- **Clasp**
- **Small beads**
- **Scissors**

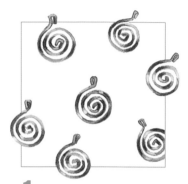

1 Make 7 spirals, following the instructions shown at left.

3 Add a spiral, string on a few more beads, then add another spiral. Repeat until you've used all the spirals. After the last one, add about 40 more beads.

To give your jewelry a **whole new spin,** add swirling silver spirals.

2 Tie a clasp section to the end of the string, then add about 40 beads.

4 Hold the choker up to your neck to see if the spirals are evenly spaced, then tie on the other clasp section. Trim any extra string.

Spiral Shower

Everyday Anklets

From parties or school to the swimming pool, you can create an anklet for any occasion! Change the style simply by using iridescent, glass, or patterned beads.

Easy Earrings

Design dainty earrings in a snap. Here's how: spin 2 spirals, add beads if desired, make end loops, and attach the end loops to your favorite style of earring wires.

Notebook Jewelry

Add color to class notebooks with paper clips! Make as many spirals as desired, then attach them to every other ring on the notebook. As an option, leave a longer tail on the spiral and add a bead or charm before making the end loop.

Zigzags

Go up and down to create these bends,
then share this project with your friends!

Cool-fetti!

Making a Zigzag

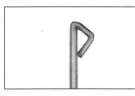

1 Straighten a paper clip, then make an end loop.

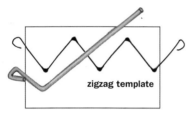

zigzag template

2 Lay the clip on the template above, and make a bend at the first dot. (You can also create your own zigzag sizes.)

3 Repeat until you've made all the bends. Finish with another end loop.

YOU WILL NEED

- **7 gold paper clips**
- **Pliers**
- **Colorful beads**
- **Clasp**

1 To make this bracelet, follow the instructions shown at left, only make uneven zigzags as seen below. Create 4 zigzags, adding beads before each bend.

Create a colorful zigzag bracelet that **rises and falls** like confetti tossed into the air!

2 Open the end loop on a zigzag, slip in another end loop, and reclose. Repeat with remaining zigzags. Adjust the end loop angles where they connect so the zigzags will lie flat.

3 Spin 3 spirals. Open a spiral's end loop, slip it on a loop where 2 clips connect, then reclose. Repeat with the remaining spirals.

4 Open the end loops to attach both sections of the clasp.

Zigzag Zone

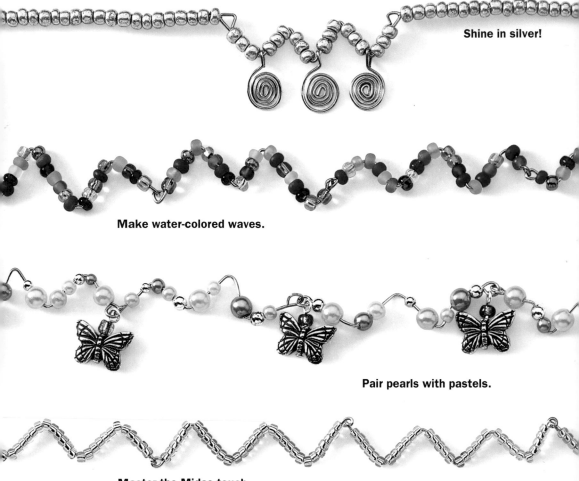

Shine in silver!

Make water-colored waves.

Pair pearls with pastels.

Master the Midas touch.

Curlicues

Curl lots of paper clips or curl just one.
Inventing ways to use them is *so much* fun!

"Y" Design!

Making a Curlicue

1 Straighten a paper clip. Add an end loop. Lay a narrow object, such as a knitting needle, across the clip.

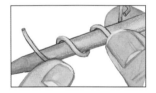

2 Holding the end loop, wrap the clip around the needle with your thumb. Remove needle.

3 Make another end loop, then position the ends at right angles to the curlicue so the jewelry lies correctly.

YOU WILL NEED

- 3 silver paper clips
- Pliers
- Knitting needle or other narrow object
- Seed beads
- Charm
- 2 feet of string
- Clasp
- Scissors

Create a **glistening Y choker** by covering paper clips and string with iridescent beads.

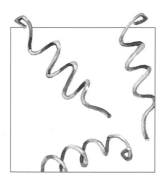

1 Make 3 curlicues, following steps 1 and 2 shown at left.

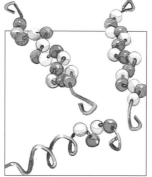

2 Fill the curlicues with beads, *then* make end loops.

3 Connect the end loops of 2 curlicues to the same loop of the third curlicue so it dangles between them to make a Y. Attach the charm to the bottom of the third curlicue.

4 Tie about 1 foot of string to each end loop. Add enough beads for the choker to fit your neck. Make sure both sides are even, then tie the string ends to the clasp. Snip extra string.

Classy Curlicues

Dressy Tresses

To perk up a ponytail, make a beaded curlicue and a spiral from plastic paper clips. Reopen both the loops on the curlicue. Attach one end to an elastic band and the other end to a spiral, then reclose. Repeat with more curlicues and spirals.

Long Curls

These dangling earrings are fun to make for Mom! Attach beaded curlicues to earring wires, and add spirals or charms to the ends.

Lamp Lights

This project is easier to do with a paper shade, but a fabric one will work, too. Use a bulletin board pushpin to poke holes in the shade about 1 inch apart and just above the bottom seam. (Keep fingers out of the path of the pushpin!) Bead a curlicue for each hole, bending an end loop on one end and a hook on the other. Slip the hook into the hole. You may need to remove curlicues and adjust them so they dangle better.

Loop-the-Loops

Go around in a circle and out the opposite way.
Slip a charm on the loop, and there it will stay!

Droplet

Making a Loop-the-Loop

1 Straighten a paper clip, then lay a knitting needle or other narrow object across it.

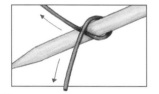

2 Use your thumbs to wrap the legs of the clip tightly around the needle until you form a complete circle. Remove the needle.

3 Make end loops. Line them up with the center loop and angle them inward, as shown above.

YOU WILL NEED

- 2 gold paper clips
- Knitting needle or other narrow object
- Pliers
- Dark and light blue beads
- 2 feet of blue string
- Marker
- Clasp

1 Make a loop-the-loop, following steps 1 and 2 shown at left. Use the other clip to make a spiral.

4 Fill the V with beads in alternating colors, then make the end loops shown in step 3 at left.

Water-colored beads seem to **trickle down golden wire** and drop onto a delicate hanging spiral.

2 Leave room to add 2 beads before the end loop. Turn the end loop at a right angle to the spiral.

3 Slide a dark bead, the spiral, then another dark bead onto the loop-the-loop.

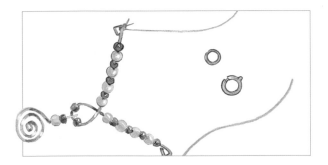

5 Tie 1 foot of string to each end loop. Hold the choker to your neck. Have someone mark where the clasp should be. Tie a clasp section to each mark. If the droplet doesn't hang straight, adjust the string.

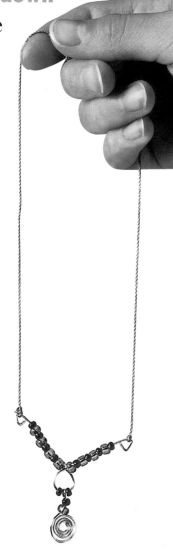

Lot-a-Loops!

Make **small variations** to wire shapes, beads, or charms to create a loop-the-loop for any occasion!

Coils

Tightly curled coils spring into action—
colorful beads are an added attraction!

Casual Coils

Making a Coil

1 Straighten a paper clip, then lay a knitting needle or other narrow object across it to form an X. Use your thumbs to wrap the legs of the clip around the needle, keeping the wraps very close together. Remove the needle.

2 Use your pliers to bend the ends of the clip in line with the rest of the coil.

YOU WILL NEED

- **15 plastic paper clips**
- **Knitting needle or other narrow object**
- **Pliers**
- **Small beads**
- **Clasp**

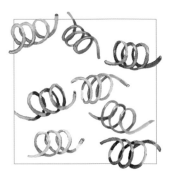

1 Make 15 coils, following step 1 shown at left.

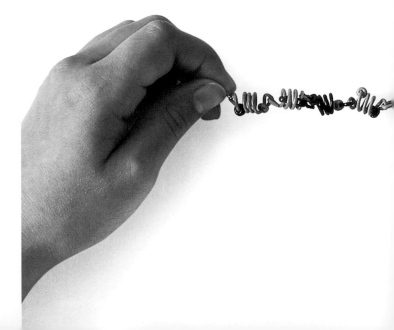

Fashion an **all-weather anklet** that's casual enough for the backyard or the beach.

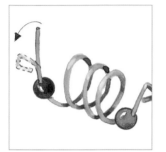

2 Slide a bead on each end, then make end loops. To help coils lie straighter when linked, bend end loops so they point out from the ends of the coil.

3 Open an end loop, slip in the end loop of another coil, then reclose. Repeat with the remaining coils.

4 Attach both sections of a clasp to the end loops.

Coil Collection

Gone Fishing

Reel in this simple but eye-catching necklace. Use a charm, beads, coils, and a chain in 3 basic colors: black, white, and silver.

Rejects Rescued!

Save your less-than-perfect coils to create this cool bracelet. String blue beads and sloppy silver coils on a leather cord. Tie closed.

Exotic Anklets

Coil up with a one-of-a-kind anklet! Create your own styles using loose or tight coils, leather cord, glass beads, mini charms, and hemp string.

Wraps

Give a plain stone a pretty wrap.
With a paper clip, it's a snap!

Making a Wrap

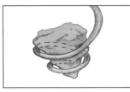

1 Straighten a paper clip, then hold it near the bottom of a small stone. Crisscross or circle the clip to keep the stone from falling out.

2 Leave enough wire to make an end loop, then slip a cord through it.

Option: Open the wrap end loop, slip in the end loop of a coil, twist, curlicue, or loop-the-loop, then reclose.

Adorn a **sparkling green stone** with a silver twist and purple beads and string.

Pastel beads make this **pretty-in-pink** heart oh so sweet!

Beautiful stones need only a **simple wrap** and silk cord.

It's a Wrap!

An **earthy** hemp string adds contrast to a golden-dressed stone.

Purple string and beads **harmonize** with a purple amethyst.

Iridescent purple beads and a golden loop-the-loop add a **hint of color** to crystal.

A zigzag and shiny beads perk up a **plain pebble.**

Turn a simple stone into a **precious jewel** using a wire wrap!

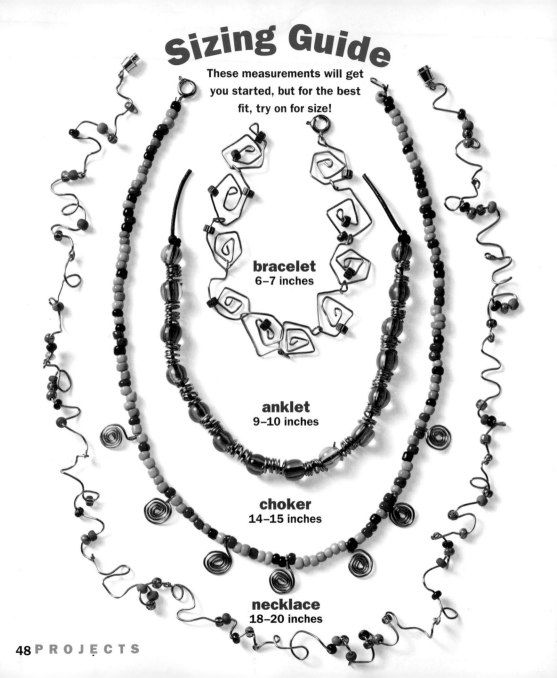

Sizing Guide

These measurements will get
you started, but for the best
fit, try on for size!

bracelet
6–7 inches

anklet
9–10 inches

choker
14–15 inches

necklace
18–20 inches

Try it risk-free!

American Girl magazine is especially for girls 8 and up. Send for your preview issue today! Mail this card to receive a risk-free preview issue and start your one-year subscription. For just $22.95, you'll receive 6 bimonthly issues in all! If you don't love it right away, just write "cancel" on the invoice and return it to us. The preview issue is yours to keep, free!

Send bill to: (please print)

Adult's name

Address

City   State   Zip

Adult's signature

Send magazine to: (please print)

Girl's name   Birth date *(optional)*

Address

City   State   Zip

Free catalogue!

Welcome to a world that's all yours—because it's filled with the things girls love! Beautiful dolls that capture your heart. Books that send your imagination soaring. And games and pastimes that make being a girl great!

For your free American Girl® catalogue, return this postcard, call 1-800-845-0005, or visit our Web site at americangirl.com.

Send me a catalogue:

Name   Girl's birth date

Address

City   State   Zip

E-mail *(Fill in to receive order information, updates, and Web-exclusive offers.)*

(   )
Phone   ☐ Home   ☐ Work

Parent's signature   12583i

Send my friend a catalogue:

Name

Address

City   State   Zip

12591i